DELAWARE

The First State

BY
JOHN HAMILTON

Abdo & Daughters
An imprint of Abdo Publishing | abdopublishing.com

abdopublishing.com

Published by ABDO Publishing, a division of ABDO, PO Box 398166, Minneapolis, Minnesota 55439. Copyright © 2017 by Abdo Consulting Group, Inc. International copyrights reserved in all countries. No part of this book may be reproduced in any form without written permission from the publisher. ABDO & Daughters™ is a trademark and logo of ABDO Publishing.

Printed in the United States of America, North Mankato, Minnesota.
012016
092016

Editor: Sue Hamilton   **Contributing Editor:** Bridget O'Brien
Graphic Design: Sue Hamilton
Cover Art Direction: Candice Keimig   **Cover Photo Selection:** Neil Klinepier
Cover Photo: iStock
Interior Images: AP, Big Barrel Country Music Festival, Corbis, Delaware 87ers, Delaware Geological Survey, Delaware State Parks, Domenick D'Andrea, Dreamstime, DuPont, Eric A. Arnold, Getty, Granger, Hargrett Rare Book & Manuscript Library-Univ of Georgia, History In Full Color-Restoration/Colorization, iStock, Library of Congress, Mile High Maps, Minden, National Atlas of the U.S., National Park Service, Penn Treaty Museum, Rob Brooks, Science Source, Scriptorium-Howard Pyle, Stanley Arthur, State of Delaware, Town of Smyrna, U.S. Air Force, U.S. Army Corps of Engineers, U.S. Department of Defense, U.S. Geological Survey, University of Delaware, White House, Wikimedia, William Weinrich, & Wilmington Blue Rocks.

Statistics: *State and City Populations*, U.S. Census Bureau, July 1, 2014 estimates; *Land and Water Area*, U.S. Census Bureau, 2010 Census, MAF/TIGER database; *State Temperature Extremes*, NOAA National Climatic Data Center; *Climatology and Average Annual Precipitation*, NOAA National Climatic Data Center, 1980-2015 statewide averages; *State Highest and Lowest Points*, NOAA National Geodetic Survey.

Websites: To learn more about the United States, visit booklinks.abdopublishing.com. These links are routinely monitored and updated to provide the most current information available.

Cataloging-in-Publication Data

Names: Hamilton, John, 1959- author.
Title: Delaware / by John Hamilton.
Description: Minneapolis, MN : Abdo Publishing, [2016] | The United States of America | Includes index.
Identifiers: LCCN 2015957508 | ISBN 9781680783100 (print) | ISBN 9781680774146 (ebook)
Subjects: LCSH: Delaware--Juvenile literature.
Classification: DDC 975.1--dc23
LC record available at http://lccn.loc.gov/2015957508

CONTENTS

THE FIRST STATE

Old State House

Delaware is the second-smallest state. Measured north and south, it is only 95 miles (153 km) long. But this little state is often called "The Small Wonder." It stands tall in United States history. After the American Revolution, in 1787, it was the first state to vote "yes" to ratify the U.S. Constitution. That is why its official nickname is "The First State."

Today, Delaware residents have higher-than-average incomes. The state's businesses are some of the most productive in the country. Small farms stand side-by-side with giant corporations. Chemical maker DuPont has been in Delaware for more than 200 years.

The state is also filled with natural beauty, from forests and wetlands to sandy beaches and rolling hills. It is no surprise people like to visit Delaware. There's something for everyone in "The Small Wonder."

People enjoy 6 miles (10 km) of white-sand beach bordering the Atlantic Ocean at Cape Henlopen State Park.

A tall ship sails past the Delaware East End Breakwater Lighthouse, just offshore from Lewes, Delaware. Established in 1885, the lighthouse sits at the end of an artificial breakwater made of 835,000 tons (757,499 metric tons) of stone.

QUICK FACTS

DECEMBER 7, 1787

Name: The state is named after the Delaware River, which got its name from Thomas West (1577-1618). He was an English nobleman and governor of colonial Virginia whose title was "Baron De La Warr."

State Capital: Dover, population 37,355

Date of Statehood: December 7, 1787 (1st state)

Population: 935,614 (45th-most populous state)

Area (Total Land and Water): 2,489 square miles (6,446 sq km), 49th-largest state

Largest City: Wilmington, population 71,817

Nickname: The First State

Motto: Liberty and Independence

State Bird: Blue Hen Chicken

State Flower: Peach Blossom

State Mineral: Sillimanite

State Tree: American Holly

State Song: "Our Delaware"

Highest Point: Ebright Azimuth, 448 feet (137 m)

Lowest Point: Atlantic Ocean, 0 feet (0 m)

Average July High Temperature: 87°F (31°C)

Record High Temperature: 110°F (43°C), in Millsboro on July 21, 1930

Average January Low Temperature: 25°F (-4°C)

Record Low Temperature: -17°F (-27°C), in Millsboro on January 17, 1893

Average Annual Precipitation: 44 inches (112 cm)

Number of U.S. Senators: 2

Number of U.S. Representatives: 1

U.S. Postal Service Abbreviation: DE

GEOGRAPHY

Delaware is the second-smallest state behind Rhode Island. Covering just 2,489 square miles (6,446 sq km), it has only three counties (New Castle in the north, Kent in the middle, and Sussex in the south). From north to south, the state is about 95 miles (153 km) long. At its narrowest, in the north, it is only 9 miles (14 km) wide. In the south, Delaware is about 35 miles (56 km) wide.

Delaware occupies the east side of the Delmarva Peninsula. Bordering Delaware to the west and south is Maryland. Pennsylvania is to the north. The Delaware River, Delaware Bay, and the Atlantic Ocean form most of the state's eastern border. Small parts of New Jersey also share Delaware's eastern border.

A tidal salt marsh attracts thousands of birds and animals at the Bombay Hook National Wildlife Refuge on the coast of Delaware Bay, near Smyrna, Delaware.

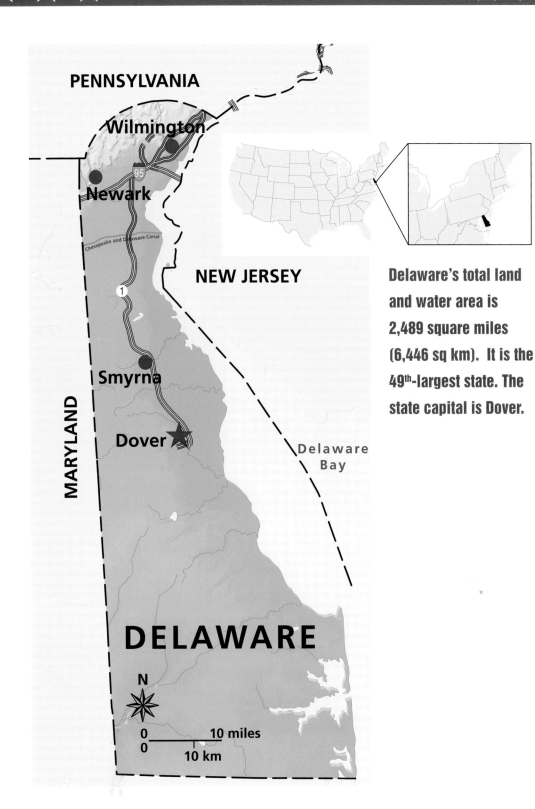

Delaware's total land and water area is 2,489 square miles (6,446 sq km). It is the 49th-largest state. The state capital is Dover.

Delaware is a mid-Atlantic state, with New England to the north and the South Atlantic states to the south. Its terrain is mostly a flat coastal plain. There are some rolling hills in the northern Piedmont region, but they barely rise 400 feet (122 m) above sea level. The state's highest point is Ebright Azimuth, north of the city of Wilmington near the Pennsylvania border. Its elevation is 448 feet (137 m) above sea level.

Delaware's busiest cities are in the north. There is much fertile farmland in the southern half of the state. Charming small towns are found throughout the countryside. Delaware has a marshy coast, but in several areas there are sandy beaches along Delaware Bay and the Atlantic Ocean.

Delaware's Cape Henlopen State Park is a beachside park bordered by Delaware Bay and the Atlantic Ocean.

A ship travels under a lift bridge on the Chesapeake and Delaware Canal in New Castle County, Delaware.

The Chesapeake and Delaware Canal cuts across the northern part of the state. It continues into Maryland before reaching Chesapeake Bay. Part of the canal is natural. Over the years, construction projects have deepened, widened, and straightened the waterway. The 14-mile (23-km) -long canal was built to make it easier for cargo ships from Baltimore, Maryland, to reach the Atlantic Ocean or Philadelphia, Pennsylvania. Without this shortcut, ships would have to travel south down the length of Chesapeake Bay. Because of the canal, ships traveling from Baltimore to Philadelphia shave almost 300 miles (483 km) off the length of their voyages.

CLIMATE AND
WEATHER

Delaware's climate is mild. It is not too cold in winter, and not too hot in summer. There is usually a lot of water vapor in the air. This humid, moderate climate is caused by the nearby Atlantic Ocean. In July, the average daily high temperature is 87°F (31°C). In January, the average low is 25°F (-4°C).

Delaware is a small state, but there is a surprising difference in climate between the northern and southern halves. The south is much more affected by the warm waters of the Atlantic Ocean. Temperatures are moderate, and there is a longer growing season for crops. Along the coast, temperatures are about 10 degrees Fahrenheit (5.6°C) warmer in winter, and 10 degrees Fahrenheit (5.6°C) cooler in summer. The north is farther away from the seashore. The weather is less steady, with bigger swings in temperature.

Residents clear snow in Hockessin, Delaware. Located in the northern part of the state, the town has greater swings in temperature than warmer southern Delaware.

A nor'easter comes ashore at Rehoboth Beach. Delaware's southern coastal areas sometimes see these storms sweep in off the warm waters of the Atlantic Ocean.

Average annual precipitation statewide is 44 inches (112 cm). Strong seasonal storms sometimes sweep into the state. In winter or spring, nor'easters can dump heavy snow or rain and cause coastal flooding. Strong thunderstorms sometimes strike in summer.

PLANTS AND
ANIMALS

Of all the states along the Atlantic Ocean seacoast, Delaware is the least forested. Europeans first arrived in the 1600s. They quickly discovered that the land could be made suitable for farming. Much forestland was cut down. Today, only about 30 percent of Delaware is forested. Most of the forested land is privately owned.

Delaware's forests have a rich mix of species. The most common trees include red maples, red oaks, loblolly pines, sweet gums, and white oaks. Loblolly pines are found in the southern forests. Along the coast grow pitch pines, red cedars, and bayberry trees. The Great Cypress Swamp is located on the southern edge of Delaware. Many bald cypress and Atlantic white cedar trees grow there.

A hardwood forest in Norman G. Wilder Wildlife Area near Viola, Delaware. The area contains more than 4,400 acres (1,781 ha) of forestland, in the central part of the state.

A stand of bald cypress trees in Trussum Pond, Sussex County, Delaware.

Grey Fox

Common animals found in Delaware's forests and meadows include deer, foxes, raccoons, skunks, and opossums. The grey fox is the official state wildlife animal. Smaller animals found in Delaware include chipmunks, squirrels, moles, and rabbits.

Many kinds of fish make their homes in Delaware's streams and ponds. They include bass, pike, and trout. The official state fish is the weakfish. It is also called sea trout. It inhabits waters all along the Atlantic Ocean coast. Swimming in Delaware Bay are bluefish, flounder, perch, and Norfolk spot. Norfolk spot are small but feisty. They have a distinctive black spot near their gills. Crabs and clams are also harvested from Delaware Bay. The official state marine animal is the horseshoe crab. Delaware Bay has more horseshoe crabs than any other place on Earth.

Horseshoe crabs live in the ocean, but come ashore every year to spawn. They arrive at Delaware Bay by the thousands between the May and June full moons.

Snapping turtles are commonly seen in Delaware's swamps and marshes. There are many snakes found statewide.

Snapping Turtle

They include hognose, garter, corn, and eastern milk snakes, as well as poisonous northern copperheads and timber rattlesnakes.

Common birds flying overhead include robins, starlings, cardinals, blue jays, and ruby-throated hummingbirds. The official state bird is the Delaware blue hen. It is a type of chicken raised on farms. Along Delaware's shores are found great blue herons, snowy egrets, sandpipers, gulls, and terns.

A pair of black-headed gulls land on a Delaware shore to feed on horseshoe crab eggs.

HISTORY

Before Europeans arrived in the 1600s, the land we now call Delaware was settled by thousands of Native Americans. In the north and central part of the state were members of the Lenni Lenape, later called the Delaware Indians. These Algonquian-speaking people lived peaceful lives hunting, fishing, and farming. In the western part of the state lived the Minqua. They were more warlike, and sometimes attacked Lenni Lenape villages. In the south lived other tribes, including the Nanticoke, Assateague, and Choptank people. After European settlers came, most of the Native Americans moved west to escape warfare and disease.

Henry Hudson meets Native Americans on the shore of Delaware Bay in 1609.

A replica of Henry Hudson's Dutch East India Company ship, Halve Maen (Half Moon).

The first Europeans to visit Delaware were probably Spanish or Portuguese explorers of the late 1500s. Henry Hudson was the first European we know for sure spotted Delaware. Hudson was English, but he worked for the Dutch East India Company. His mission was to explore the New World. In 1609, he and his group of explorers sailed into Delaware Bay and partway up the Delaware River. In the decade that followed, other explorers mapped the Delaware coastline.

In 1631, twenty-eight Dutch settlers landed and began a settlement near today's Lewes, Delaware. They established a colony called Zwaanendael. The settlers fought with local Native Americans. By 1632, the colonists were killed and the settlement burned.

In 1631, Dutch settlers arrived along the southern coast of Delaware. They built a fort near today's town of Lewes. They called their settlement Zwaanendael, which means "valley of the swans." They wanted to farm and trade. Unfortunately, the newcomers fought with local Native Americans. The Dutch were killed and the settlement was destroyed.

People from Sweden founded the first permanent settlement in Delaware. In 1638, they started a colony called New Sweden. They built a trading post at Fort Christina, near present-day Wilmington.

After the Swedish people established their colony, Delaware went through a tug-of-war between several countries. They all wanted to control the area, which was good for farming and fur trading. In 1651, the Dutch returned. Four years later, they took over New Sweden. Just nine years after that, in 1664, a fleet of British ships arrived. The British took the settlement away from the Dutch.

During the 1776 Battle of Long Island, the 1ˢᵗ Delaware Regiment fought beside the 1ˢᵗ Maryland. The well-equipped Delaware Blues and the Marylanders helped prevent the capture of the majority of George Washington's Continental Army.

Finally, in 1682, Pennsylvania Governor William Penn found himself in control of the Delaware area. He allowed the people of Delaware to make their own laws. In 1776, Delaware declared its independence from Pennsylvania. Later that same year, the 13 American colonies declared independence from Great Britain. About 4,000 soldiers from Delaware fought during the American Revolution.

During the Revolutionary War, the British army occupied the Delaware city of Wilmington. Much of the British navy was anchored in Delaware Bay. After many years of fighting, the United States won its independence from Great Britain in 1783. In 1787, Delaware became the first state to approve, or ratify, the United States Constitution.

During the 1800s, Delaware's economy grew. The state has many swift-flowing streams and rivers, which powered mills and factories. Ships had easy access to the Atlantic Ocean. Busy Philadelphia, Pennsylvania, was just a short trip up the Delaware River. In 1829, the Chesapeake and Delaware Canal opened for business. It was a good shortcut for ships. The first railroads were built in the state in the 1830s. Railroads made it even easier for Delaware businesses to transport goods.

During the Civil War (1861-1865), Delaware did not join the South's Confederacy. Even though Delaware was a slave state, it stayed in the Union. There was much division in the state over slavery. By the time the war started, there were less than 1,800 slaves in Delaware.

Philadelphia, Baltimore and Washington Railroad train cars wait to take on loads of watermelons from farmers in Laurel, Delaware, in 1905.

Delaware's swift-flowing streams and rivers powered the equipment used in many of the state's mills and factories.

In modern times, Delaware's population has shifted. Many people have moved to Wilmington and its suburbs. Laws passed in the 1980s made it easier for big companies to move their headquarters to Delaware, which greatly helped the state's economy.

DID YOU KNOW?

- Most states have borders that are straight, or follow the path of a river or large body of water. Delaware's unusual northern border is shaped like a semicircle. It follows an arc that extends 12 miles (19 km) from the courthouse in the town of New Castle. This part of Delaware's border is often called the Twelve-Mile Circle. It is the only circle-shaped border in the United States.

- The record low temperature ever recorded in Delaware was -17°F (-27°C) on January 17, 1893. The record high was 110°F (43°C) on July 21, 1930. Both occurred in the town of Millsboro, in the southern part of the state near the Atlantic Ocean coast.

Delaware State Parks
We're saving a place for you

- Delaware is the only state with no national parks. However, it does have 17 state parks. The National Recreation and Park Association (NRPA) awarded Delaware State Parks with the 2016 National Gold Medal Award for Excellence in Park and Recreation Management.

- In 1776, Caesar Rodney was one of Delaware's three delegates to the Continental Congress. The other two delegates split their vote in deciding whether Delaware would support the Declaration of Independence. To break the tie, Rodney rode 70 miles (113 km) through a thunderstorm, from Dover, Delaware, to Philadelphia, Pennsylvania, to cast his vote. Thanks to Rodney, Delaware officially supported independence from Great Britain.

- Thomas Garrett (1789-1871) was an important Underground Railroad stationmaster. Before the Civil War, he moved to Wilmington, Delaware, and helped runaway slaves hide from the authorities. He hid them in his home and gave them food, money, and clothing. Garrett was a friend of Harriet Tubman. He said he helped about 2,700 slaves find freedom.

PEOPLE

Joe Biden (1942-) was the 47th vice president of the United States. He served two terms under President Barack Obama. Biden was born in Scranton, Pennsylvania, but moved to Delaware when he was 10 years old. He graduated from the University of Delaware in 1965. After earning his law degree, he served on the New Castle County Council. He also started his own law firm. At age 29, he became the second-youngest person ever elected to the United States Senate.

Biden represented Delaware in the Senate for 36 years. He became an expert on criminal justice, foreign policy, women's rights, and terrorism. In 2009 he became vice president of the United States, where he served for eight years.

Éleuthère-Irénée du Pont (1771-1834) was a chemist and businessman. He founded the DuPont Company. He was born in France, but came to America in 1800. He settled in northern Delaware in 1802, near Wilmington. Du Pont realized that American gunpowder used in firearms and cannons was of poor quality. He started a factory that produced superior gunpowder. His company was very important during the War of 1812. Large government contracts helped the factory grow. Du Pont died in 1834, near the town of Greenville. His company continued to expand. It eventually produced many kinds of chemicals, medicines, and other goods. Today, the company has factories all over the world, but its headquarters remains in Delaware.

Annie Jump Cannon (1863-1941) spent her adult life studying the stars and finding ways to classify them. Born the daughter of U.S. Senator Wilson Cannon from Delaware, she grew up in Dover. In college, she studied physics, math, and astronomy. She became an astronomer at Harvard College Observatory in 1896. During her long career, she classified more than 358,000 stars. She helped create a way of categorizing stars by analyzing their light. Called the Harvard spectral classification scheme, it describes stars based on their temperature. Cannon won many honors for her work. Few women at the time chose scientific careers. She accomplished much in her life, despite being almost completely deaf.

Howard Pyle (1853-1911) was one of the most successful and influential artists of the late 1800s and early 1900s. He was born and grew up in Wilmington, Delaware. He studied art at an early age, encouraged by his mother. He drew illustrations for magazines, and murals for public exhibit. But he was most famous for his illustrated children's books. They included *The Merry Adventures of Robin Hood* and *The Story of King Arthur and His Knights*. He also drew pictures for many pirate stories. Pyle taught at his art school in Wilmington. He liked to help young artists. Among his famous students were N.C. Wyeth and Elenore Abbott.

CITIES

Wilmington is Delaware's largest city. Its population is 71,817. It was founded in 1638, near the site of Fort Christina, the Swedish fort that was the first permanent settlement in Delaware. Wilmington is located in the northern tip of the state. It lies along the banks of the Christina and Delaware Rivers. It is between the cities of Philadelphia, Pennsylvania, to the northeast, and Baltimore, Maryland, to the southwest.

Wilmington is a center for manufacturing. It is also home to many finance and insurance companies, thanks to Delaware laws that are friendly to businesses. City residents enjoy music festivals, a zoo, museums, plus art galleries such as the Delaware Art Museum.

Legislative Hall

Dover's Old State House

Dover Air Force Base

Dover is the state capital of Delaware. It is located in the middle of the state, not far from Delaware Bay. It was founded in 1683. Today, its population is 37,355. It is the second-largest city in Delaware.

Many people in Dover work for the state government. In addition, the city is home to Dover Air Force Base, an important military air freight terminal. Tourists like to visit the city's many historic buildings. Residents enjoy performances by local opera, symphony, and theater companies. NASCAR races are held at Dover International Speedway. Delaware State University and Wesley College are located in Dover.

University of Delaware

Newark is Delaware's third-largest city. It began in the early 1700s as a mill town that also served travelers. It was originally named New Ark. Today, its population is 33,008. It is located in the northwest corner of the state, along the Maryland border. Newark has many historic buildings downtown. It has a small-town feel, but with many modern touches. It is friendly to industry and small businesses. It has a well-developed park and trail system, plus music and food festivals. Newark is also home to the University of Delaware, which enrolls more than 20,000 students. The university is well known for its chemical engineering and business programs.

Smyrna Market Street Plaza

Lake Como

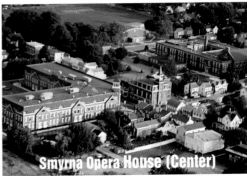

Smyrna Opera House (Center)

Smyrna is in central Delaware, just north of Dover. Settled in the early 1700s, the tiny hamlet was first known as Duck Creek. It became famous as a shipbuilding center. Today, the city has a population of 11,170. It has a historic small-town atmosphere, with many buildings dating back to the 1700s. More than 490 buildings qualify for the National Register of Historic Places. The Smyrna Opera House has been entertaining and informing people for almost 150 years. It is a community performing arts center that also houses an art gallery. Popular outdoor activities include swimming and boating in Lake Como, or hiking and bird watching in Bombay Hook, a national wildlife refuge just east of town.

TRANSPORTATION

Only one major interstate highway goes through Delaware. Interstate 95 travels southwest to northeast through the northern part of the state. It is the main link between Delaware and neighboring big cities such as Philadelphia, Pennsylvania, and Baltimore, Maryland. Several other U.S. and state highways crisscross Delaware. The main route connecting the capital city of Dover to larger cities in the north is Delaware Route 1. In total, the state has about 6,400 miles (10,300 km) of public roadways.

Delaware's first railroads were built in the 1830s. Today, Delaware has about 300 miles (483 km) of tracks still running in the state. They include both freight and passenger lines.

Drivers on Delaware Route 1 near Smyrna, Delaware. This main route connects the capital city of Dover to Delaware's larger northern cities.

Port of Wilmington

The Port of Wilmington is the busiest terminal on the Delaware River. It is a deepwater port that handles about 400 ships and 6 million tons (5.4 million metric tons) of cargo each year. In addition to cargo ships, there are two ferries that shuttle people along the Delaware River and Delaware Bay. Woodland Ferry, in southwest Delaware, is one of the oldest cable ferries in the United States. It began moving people across the Nanticoke River in the 1740s.

Delaware's busiest public airport is New Castle Airport, just south of Wilmington. It serves mainly private aircraft. A larger airport is Dover Air Force Base. It handles huge amounts of military cargo.

New Castle Airport

NATURAL
RESOURCES

Delaware's coastal plains hold vast quantities of Greenwich soil. It is deep, and drains water well. It is very productive for farming and forestry. Much of the southern part of Delaware is used for farming. More than 2,300 farms are in the state. They mostly grow corn and soybeans. Some farmers also grow fruits and vegetables, including tomatoes, melons, peas, and apples. Most of Delaware's grain crop is used as chicken feed. Broiler chickens are the state's most important agricultural product. Delaware farmers raise more than 200 million birds each year. They are sold all over the United States and in countries around the world.

Chickens are Delaware's most important agricultural product.

Commercial fishermen sort oysters brought up from Delaware Bay.

Off Delaware's eastern shores, commercial fishermen haul in millions of pounds of seafood each year. Caught in the waters of Delaware Bay and the Atlantic Ocean are blue crabs, clams, and oysters. Important fish include black sea bass, striped bass, and weakfish.

Delaware has a small number of mines. Magnesium, sand, gravel, and crushed stone are the most important products. A small amount of gemstones are also pulled from the Earth.

Delaware mines produce sand, gravel, and crushed stone.

NATURAL RESOURCES

INDUSTRY

The northern part of Delaware is close to big cities on the East Coast, such as Philadelphia, Pennsylvania, and Baltimore, Maryland. Delaware has grown to become a manufacturing center to supply these big cities. Most of the state's industry is in the Wilmington area.

Delaware is often called "The Chemical Capital of the World." DuPont has been headquartered in the state for more than 200 years. It is one of the largest chemical companies in the world. Other chemical companies in Delaware include Ashland, Dow, and BASF. Together, these companies make products such as paint, nylon, dyes, medicines, and biofuels. Dover, in the middle of the state, is also an industrial center. It is home to many food-processing companies. Other manufactured goods important to Delaware include paper, plastic, transportation equipment, and electronic products.

DuPont has offices around the world, but the company's headquarters have been in Delaware for more than 200 years.

In recent years, Delaware passed laws making it easier for banks and other companies to do business in the state. Taxes are low and courts are set up to understand complex financial issues. As a result, many companies make Delaware their corporate headquarters, even if their main offices and factories are in other states. Almost half of all United States companies have their corporate headquarters in Delaware.

The southern part of Delaware, especially the Atlantic Ocean seacoast, has many wildlife areas and resorts. Tourism is big business in this part of the state.

Rehoboth Beach is a popular tourist destination. Delaware has some of the cleanest beaches in the United States. The Natural Resources Defense Council rated Delaware #1 in beach water quality in 2013.

SPORTS

There are no major league professional football, baseball, basketball, or hockey teams in Delaware. Most people are fans of teams in neighboring cities, such as Philadelphia, Pennsylvania, Baltimore, Maryland, or Washington, D.C. However, there are several minor league teams in the state. They include the Wilmington Blue Rocks (baseball) and the Delaware 87ers (basketball).

Many people in Delaware are big fans of the football team at the University of Delaware, in Newark. Other university sports teams are also popular.

Fans of the University of Delaware Fightin' Blue Hens football team attend home games at Delaware Stadium in Newark, Delaware.

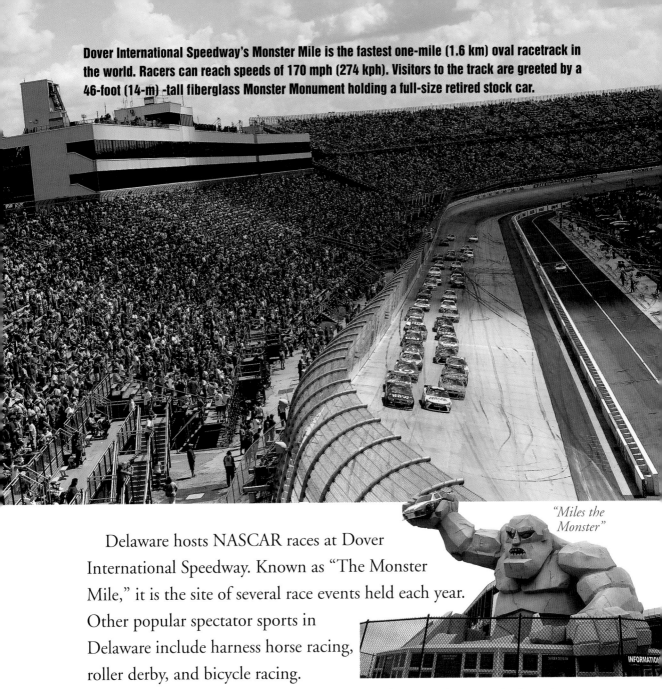

Dover International Speedway's Monster Mile is the fastest one-mile (1.6 km) oval racetrack in the world. Racers can reach speeds of 170 mph (274 kph). Visitors to the track are greeted by a 46-foot (14-m) -tall fiberglass Monster Monument holding a full-size retired stock car.

"Miles the Monster"

Delaware hosts NASCAR races at Dover International Speedway. Known as "The Monster Mile," it is the site of several race events held each year. Other popular spectator sports in Delaware include harness horse racing, roller derby, and bicycle racing.

Outdoor lovers can find many things to do in Delaware. Swimming, fishing, and boating are popular along the coast or inland lakes and rivers. In the state's parks and forests, people can hike or watch wildlife. The largest state park in Delaware is Redden State Forest, in the southern part of the state. Its loblolly pine forests are laced with paths for hiking, bicycling, and horseback riding.

SPORTS

ENTERTAINMENT

Visitors to Delaware enjoy the many old, historic buildings in small towns throughout the state. Many were built as far back as the 1600s. The Holy Trinity Church in Wilmington is a National Historic Landmark. Also known as Old Swedes Church, it was built in 1698 by some of Delaware's earliest pioneers. In New Castle, the Dutch House dates back to about 1700. The John Dickinson Plantation, near Dover, was built in 1740. Dover Days is a festival that celebrates the historic homes in the city each spring. Dover is also home to several major music festivals. The Big Barrel Country Music Festival and Firefly Music Festival bring top performers to Delaware.

Andrew McMahon

Carrie Underwood

Paul McCartney

The *Kalmar Nyckel* is a replica of a Swedish ship that brought settlers to the Delaware area in 1638.

The Delaware Museum of Natural History, in Greenville, has exhibits featuring dinosaurs, mammals, birds, and undersea creatures. The Winterthur Museum features American decorative arts. Founded by Henry Francis du Pont, it includes a research library and a 60-acre (24-ha) garden.

Other museums include the Delaware Art Museum, the Delaware History Museum, and the Hagley Museum and Library, all in Wilmington. The *Kalmar Nyckel* is a replica of a ship that brought early Swedish settlers to Delaware. It is a floating classroom that can be found on the Christina River in Wilmington.

The Delaware State Fair is held each July in Harrington. Wilmington hosts the Delaware Shakespeare Festival during the summer months. The city is also home to the DuPont Clifford Brown Jazz Festival, a free concert series held each June.

TIMELINE

Pre-1600s—The Lenni Lenape, Minqua, Nanticoke, Assateague, and Choptank Native American tribes occupy today's Delaware.

Henry Hudson

1609—Explorer Henry Hudson sails partway up the Delaware River.

1631—The Dutch settle near the modern-day city of Lewes, Delaware.

1638—A Swedish colony is established at Fort Christina, near modern-day Wilmington.

1651—Dutch Director-General Peter Stuyvesant establishes Fort Casimir at modern-day New Castle, Delaware.

Peter Stuyvesant

1655—The Dutch take over the Swedish colony at Fort Christina.

William Penn

1664—The British remove Dutch settlers.

1682—William Penn takes over the leadership of Delaware.

1776—Delaware declares independence from Pennsylvania.

1776—American colonies declare their independence from Great Britain.

1787—Delaware becomes the first state to ratify the United States Constitution.

1802—DuPont Powder Mill is built on the banks of Brandywine Creek near Wilmington, Delaware.

1861—The beginning of the American Civil War.

1917—The beginning of World War I for the United States. Many new immigrants arrive in Delaware.

1941—The beginning of World War II for the United States. Construction begins on Dover Air Force Base.

1980s—Laws make it easier for big companies to move their headquarters to Delaware.

2001—Delaware elects its first female governor, Ruth Ann Minner.

2009 & 2013—Joe Biden, former Delaware senator, is sworn in as vice president of the United States.

 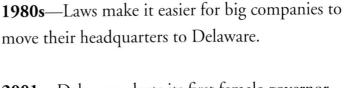

GLOSSARY

Chesapeake and Delaware Canal

A waterway that cuts across part of Maryland and Delaware. It leads from Chesapeake Bay to Delaware Bay. The canal makes it much easier for ships going to and from Baltimore, Maryland, to connect to Wilmington, Delaware, and Philadelphia, Pennsylvania, or the Atlantic Ocean.

Civil War

The war fought between America's Northern and Southern states from 1861-1865. The Southern states were for slavery. They wanted to start their own country. Northern states fought against slavery and a division of the country.

Colony

A group of people who settle in a distant territory but remain citizens of their native country.

Confederacy

The Southern states of Alabama, Arkansas, Florida, Georgia, Louisiana, Mississippi, North Carolina, South Carolina, Tennessee, Texas, and Virginia. These states broke away from the United States during the Civil War and formed their own country known as the Confederate States of America, or simply the Confederacy.

Delmarva Peninsula

The peninsula where Delaware is located. The Delmarva Peninsula also is home to parts of Maryland and Virginia.

Greenwich Soil
A deep, brown soil found in Delaware that drains water well and is very good for growing crops. It is Delaware's official state soil.

Lenni Lenape Indians
A Native American tribe that lived in Delaware before the arrival of the Europeans. The Europeans later named this tribe the "Delaware Indians."

New World
The areas of North, Central, and South America, as well as islands near these land masses. The term was often used by European explorers.

Nor'easter
Large storms that pass along the Atlantic Ocean coasts, striking the mid-Atlantic and New England states and Canadian Atlantic coast provinces. Strong winds blow from the northeast, which is why the storms are called "nor'easters."

Peninsula
An area of land with water on three sides.

Ratify
To sign or give formal agreement to a document such as a treaty, contract, or constitution. Delaware was the first state to ratify the United States Constitution in 1787.

Revolutionary War
The war fought between the American colonies and Great Britain from 1775-1783. It is also known as the American Revolution or the War of Independence.

INDEX